[G A T E S]

[GATES]

Sahar Muradi

Black
Lawrence
Press

Black
Lawrence
Press

www.blacklawrence.com

Executive Editor: Diane Goettel
Chapbook Editor: Kit Frick
Book Design: Amy Freels
Cover Design: Yolandi Oosthuizen
Cover art: "Gates" by Yolandi Oosthuizen. Used with permission.

Published 2017 by Black Lawrence Press.
Printed in the United States.

For my father, Ali, across the chasm

CONTENTS

(by first line)

[ ]

The one that belonged to her
The one where the light hit for the first time
The one between our houses
The one I crawled through to sleep on his chest
The one the dog squeezed through
The one at three over the candle and cake
The one at three at the checkpoint
The one between the earth and the sky, the refrigerator with wings
The one where he met us after one year and was a stranger
The one at the park, the one at Up Park, the one at Down Park
The one that pierced my face and they pointed and laughed
The one that took them away from me in a tube and sent them back to me
    tired
The one he went through, hairs shooting out
The one she went through, blood turning up
The one we all went through to get to the blinking lights with the cherries
The ones we put up when she was born
The ones we passed to leave for good
The ones we paid quarters to get through
The one they learned the names of Presidents for
The ones they needed social security numbers for
The one I touched in the dark of my room
The ones we couldn't talk about, ever
The one we had to close behind us to stay in, to keep neat, to not be
    tempted
The one we tried to jump and failed
The one he jumped and wasn't forgiven

The ones in the books that made animals of us

The ones that told us who we weren't

The ones that hurt, that swung and cut and rattled long after they left

The ones that kept flowers

The one I went through to go north, to go abroad, to go east, to find my
　　cardinal ways

The one she went through too tired to find her way

The one they have chosen to give them purpose

The different one I have chosen

The one I haven't yet found

The one I am looking through now with the narrow slots and passages
　　unseen

[ ]

It's a place to live,
he said
looking out over the cranes
frozen in the sand
like seagulls with still wings

There was the glass whale
standing up in the water
a dolphin facing God

There was the cigarette skyline
blank-faced buildings
tall, white, and widowed
or blue and mirrored
hundreds of them
vacant
beaded gloriously gold at night

In between were low cubes of stores
car dealerships, jewelers
and invisible trades

There were shopping malls
with arches and sea life
supermarkets built for disasters

There were convention centers and expos
and festivals that began at sunset

There were museums for other places

There was the old city
with stout white blocks
bleeding with short brown men
who worked construction

There was sudden grass
bougainvillea on the walls
hyacinths in the sand
miles of manicured walks
blue ones and red ones
black-eyed peacocks
and falcons perched on covered hands

There was no trash

There were cars and cars and cars
big tires for the dunes
diamond caps for the night
and boys like him
laughing behind sealed glass

Everywhere
a cape of fine azure
Tall men and women
in white cotton
and black rayon

men with sinful watches
women with silver faces
who loved to shop

There was fresh fruit
bottled water
expats
pilgrims
and prayer on the side of the road

There was refrigeration

There was the Qasba
with its French seats
and flat desserts
a Ferris wheel called The Eye

We went up
and in the glow of the city
before I could say it,
he said,
this is where I grew up

[ ]

Kabul
There was once. I remember. I think it must have been there. Just imagine.

Bamiyan
I climbed your two vacuums and lost my breath. But I did not cry, seeing the women in the field balance pots on their wisdom bumps.

Wardak
Malalai was taking me home. "There will be apple orchards," she said. "And fighting," laughed the driver, who was armed. I told him I was not scared, as we hemmed the narrow mountainside to the sound of something I could not name.

Paghman
There is no explanation for it. No science or natural law. The story goes that if you take a single brick from this city, no scorpion will ever bite you. Father says, we kept ours with your mother's gold.

Mazar
1
Just stepping into the square, into the standing blue pool under the pulse of a thousand white wings, something happened. Something loosened, fell, or passed through me: a precision, a shudder, lightning, vivid as a heartbreak.

2

It's true, I had a crush on the *malang* at the shrine, who marched in rags
and tassels with a tail of children, calling, "Allah hu, Allah hu, Allah hu."
His hand never extended, but all of him untethered.

3

Better than a man: *tarashak* on a hot a day.

Qargha

1

We were three in the back in black scarves that were dusted white by the
time we got there. And seeing the old hotel for the first time in twenty-five
years, father, whose corners are always straight, confessed a drunken
boyhood.

2

Please don't tell anyone that we left work early that day and drove to the
lake and ate kabobs and sour cherries and I lowered my scarf, being one
with two beards and families peppered about and joy still in bad taste that I
tried to be small, but there was the water just like that, wide and rare and
like Florida, a clear sheet of possibility, and the whisper started, the itch
spread, and grew and ballooned, and before I knew it—I leapt in—with
everything on and with all abandon.

Panjsher

1

The difference between a poem and a lion is an alphabet. The difference
between five poems and five lions is slight.

2

We walk to the hilltop that watches over the valley. We remove our shoes and continue to water his hands, now that he is under a green hat.

3

We creep past the stones marked white for mines. We kneel and spread out our picnic. An ant, a shoe, a rocket—all of it suddenly level.

[ ]

father is on the tongue
of the sewing machine
above him a plastic placemat
of fish a pink one
a pinker
a black and white

just gonna lift you a little
Tom says
like we do everyday

typical fish

his hands on his
hips and heaves
father's naked accent

Tom used to live in New York City

used to work in the market
used to stuff them with rocks
so they'd weigh more
so the women would pay more

in the Village to be exact

father's two stickers
two black glyphs
x's or t's or what's that
number just right and left
of your bone hive
two eyes on the plastic waterfall

the Israelis are dropping
leaflets
let's leave
Tom says before

father's a channel
of peppercorns
bisected by a green line
on a skewer of time

is Veselka's still there

in a screen the size of a village
someone is lying still

know what the safest street is 3rd Street know why

we couldn't get the picture
so we took NPR down Haverhill
right into the parking lot of St. Mary's
FOX at the waiting room

I heard weighting room
he heard fish scales
but we couldn't get the picture

father asked me if I knew what it meant
Peshmerga

Tom lined him up exactly
x's and o's and oh we had better go
for peace was dropping

your father's a good man they don't make anymore

fish eyes
for when you cry

no I didn't know

in the waiting room
father dubbed the glyphs
peh yaw sheen meem ray gawf hay
pesh for early
merga for death

Hell's Angels that's why

[ ]

1

Who is this boy in the bone sac asking what to do? See his thin kite
whipping. Trembling skin over his eyes. What is he asking that we should
know? Young grass at his feet.

Suppose the king is a failing leaf. His wife a blade of glass.

What should I do, she asks, rattling.

2

Once, on the tarmac, among the cadavers of green tanks, military planes,
the mountains encircling them, he kissed the black earth. It had been
twenty-five years. Time hurried down his face. Clear, not clear, clear. Men
elbowing over the bags. Here, brother, let me. One came smoothly, is that
you, my brother, do you remember me, I am in a bad way. Again he became
a boy caught by the weather, gave his arms, handed out his eyes, and kissed
the stranger with a golden bill.

3

Let her be a boat. And the sea dark, rummaging.

4

Bending to tie her lace, she is halved by the dialogue between pearls. Let her be a boat within a boat: two boats spilling water.

5

Peonies trapped in their pink fists, each of the three daughters had different faces. Their eyes sounded.

One sent invitations the color of fatigue, one prodded the door with science, one stayed on the shore,

singing *I have a mother better than a blade of grass / friends better than flowing water*

6

He placed his faith neatly in a handshake that belonged to a body outside of him. What can you do you for me. Please, she asked, what can do you for him. And swallowed her pearls. Two sacs rattling.

The handshake had done something before for him. Had built a cathedral made of calendars. Three hundred thousand pages held his body up. The way the sun glinted, you could not see the words.

Take away the enormous seeing. Please.

7

They go to the shrine, tie the cloth, distribute the flour, stand alongside a mother beating her chest, a child with two unused snakes, eyes rolling inside, a black box, seven circles, the desert, water to the elbows, barefoot, head to the stone.

The screen, a window, half legible, enter the girls.

8

Who is this soft peach in a Hurricanes cap, glasses begging for an arrow? Doesn't he know? When he shares his skeleton, a blackbird with red wings becomes a red-winged blackbird.

9

Neither had learned to swim, all those years on the peninsula. When the storms came rattling, they would shutter the windows and squeeze into the closet.

They would fasten to the radio.

[ ]

It's a matter of pulling my hat over my yes.
Not unlike shearing a wooden animal.

I have a balloon I am unwilling to let go.
I've been known to hurt adults out of the past.

If I don't say yellow, they'll think blue.
Therapy advised moving the corners of the box.

Refuge in nature that has different eyes.
Refuge in the green climb of houseplants.

In the sugar face of the moon.
In a power greater than a ten-tongued lily.

No one admits there are no saving words.
Wall Street named for a wall to keep the natives out.

Gardens have become serious.
Butterflies have become serious.

The monk advised to not turn away, to hold my seat.
There never being apples at the hardware store.

A drop in the glass can kill us but not a drop in the ocean.
Our work is to enlarge the container, he said.

When they ask me how my dad is doing I hate them.
I haven't asked my dad how he's doing.

My presence on the World Wide Web commanded nothing.
A credenza of words and gooseflesh.

He said we have much to be grateful for.
As in one can't then say anything.

Patriotism, or that he loves me exactly as I am.
If only he would change, I would be okay.

Will there be tomatoes in the garden?
Will there be a garden in the garden?

Imagine the whole thing until it diffuses.
When you re-enter reality, it will soften its beak.

Put the cap on the toothpaste, wipe around the sink.
This is not a zoo without constraint.

Ladies and gentlemen, the whips please!
Twenty lashes for not texting back.

I will wear my wounds in chapters.
I will use the Internet to build a home.

Who gave their life most?
Who fought the longest, the hardest, for like ever?

My body in the waiting room of public medicine.
No one cares where you have to be.

Noting the jade leaf that cracked and did not fall.
I woke with chiclets of dreams.

I am not real. I am just like you.
If you were real, you would have some status among nations.

All the little birds feed from the same bowl.
Everyone uses the world, I mean the word problematic.

I will have to apologize repeatedly, remedially.
I will have to collect invasions for my taxes.

This bulb is good for the environment and bad for you.
Everyone has their *thing*.

When her red reddens, my flame dims.
Did you use your container, he asked.

His teeth are out of him: he is a quince on a cane.
It was adequate, said the doctor, of the other doctor's surgery.

Dad used a paring knife for over thirty minutes.
A witch came into being.

She entered the train holding her baby and a magic marker sign.
Something pointed to our treasury being liquid.

[ ]

In the glass
of a house
made quiet
shortleaf pines
watch her
come up
on legs
a headless calf

groping the table
breathless
watches
her mother magazine
in hand
smash the wasp
black
against the glass

[ ]

Salaam alaikum
Once, when I was a girl

I ni sógóma
I believed in morning,
like a hot, yellow apple

Manda nabasheyn
We never tired. Father said,
God is good

Héré sira
We slept in twos and threes

Famil chatoor ast
It was a matter of everyone

Sómógó bédi
Someone had work, someone didn't
Someone always offered something

Owlada khoob astan
We were kids but we knew everything
We belonged to everyone

I sigi na
After prayer, there was tea
After tea, there was fruit

Befarmayen
Mother taught us to draw our feet
To let others go first

Aw ni tile
In time, day gave way to night

Jan e tan jor ast
Someone would show up asking for my body
Then another

I dógó cé ka kéné
We would exchange brothers
who were not our brothers

Khudaya shukur
The earth met us in different ways
For some, it rained
For others, there wasn't water for the stones

A barika Allah ye
We thanked God for blessing us
and not our neighbors

Khuda hafez
History was the first to leave
and without a trace

Aw ni wula
Father said the night has hands
Mother reminded me of the apple

Shab bakhair
In the dark
I held nothing

[ ]

a word is legged,
            armed

to *retreat*, move back
from a forward or threatened position
            as in chess, a piece

to *withdraw*, leave
to remove or take away
            as in love

"the whole country being a swamp
            a labor of time and utility"
            (Lady Sale, Caboul, 1842)

the longest war
            the definition
of a quagmire
            (Washington, 170 years later)

the going into
and coming out of
            a home
            a body

as in a bog

she noted, "remarkable
from having a few trees
              and a grave or two under them"

citing Alexander
              & co.
late books, headlines
              "The Graveyard of Empires"

as in literature
a pretty banner

              in a village called
The Husbandless
              "we were heavily fired upon"

which is "a curious complex"
              said Brzezinski
"they don't like foreigners with guns
 in their country"

as in
              someone must

[ ]

We flew out of San Jose and you
told me about the butterfly farm.
You said they only live between a
few hours and a month. That they
weave cocoons of golden thread,
which look like a lady's earring.
That when they drop it, the first
thing they do is defecate. That they
already know how to fly. That their
bright colors rub off on your hand
like a lady's eye shadow. That the
monarch's orange color is poison.
You said, can you believe it, you see
them and you never think.

We flew over Cuba and I told you
about the butterfly farm. I said
they only live an hour.
That they weave cocoons of
invisible thread, which look like
nothing. That when they drop it,
the first thing they do is submit.
That they already know how to
survive. That their bright colors
rubbed off like a lady's lipstick.
That the subject's orange color is
poison. I said, can you believe it,
you don't see them so you never
think about them.

[ ]

Funny organs
Bleed the same
Ache discordantly

I saw the numbers
Near half a million
Red black and green

They didn't tremble
Didn't catch their jaws
Fountain from a soft place

No, I saw them swell
White white white
Red and blue

I saw them burst
Upon a scale that sounds
A life a light worth

It hurt both ways—
Coloring bars and
Othering costs

[ ]

We have lorded over nature. Buried experiences in the Philippines among survivors. Climate lines are down. Mud and abduction. When I'm awake I move low, I sink into fundamentalism.

We freezed in the cooler of something other than cold. Dashed. It came like an oceanic disaster. Islands of finance and religion. No license. No capital. We may be sitting on seawater dying.

Science plotted. Pipe staffers wrestled money made of barely. Left the house vulnerable by men. We million celebrated, we sweltered to see him white robe among the devastated.

He believes his son loves. Lives. Live, live son. Montana poisons its people. The site of my supreme vows. Another son makes a gesture of peace for the cameras. We are safer if we are all.

Morning war. A sunset perhaps. We spent the equivalent of truth and no one caught on. Aiding an apology I didn't mean to. We demand choice to quietly obtain a breath through a wall.

Mali appeared and something softened in my union. Mr. Members of the Country, we are fifteen years into 100. Help us in our people everywhere ideology. We are air values that none can see.

English that speaks of suffering once gilded. I'd like to be caroled by a holy man. He said he believes I'm responsible. It's my fault, I slept with nature. He's my lord. I went too far with him.

Parted his hair with my two brown fingers. We authored poorer nations with the hope of freeing others. The architects of what's left. His eyes blued in the screen. A wave of exceptional secrecy.

[ ]

Tell us about your violence and its relativism. Amidst the drones I've
unwed. A baby, over 200,000 perhaps. Bodies cannot be Presidents. A
borrowed language written by the period.

A father, his father, blossomed out of a car. Petals showered. The system
raised its limbs. An attempted spiritual skyline. Tell the parents nothing.
30 years made no difference. Every day.

Recall the trinity of the goose, the garden, the legal system. My neighbor
exchanged fire with the *the*'s on the ground. Secretary weather forward
slash transitional. I want to be. Erupted into.

I was born to be 24, sunny. Mostly a flurry. An upper teen that feels like 0. I
beg the countries. Consider when the gardens are worthy. I want power to
negotiate infants one and two days old.

Leaders accused soon of late and late of soon. Addressing a joint session of
plenty. I'm asking you to be historic English. Visit us in our homes. Dug up
from the dirt after prayer. Angels.

Bring them home. Language a letter to disinvite the funeral from the
merry-go-round. Parents plea one flower after another. On-air experts of
June, we see fewer people live than ever before.

[ ]

I.

most of the tragedy happens
offstage an arm
a leg exploded cinema

in the old city
poets run their fingers
through the film

it is a double picture
the arm, the leg
then cinematic

white space
dismembering what mothers
re-member

II.

In the flow of what's happening, the Director of Language and Thinking
reconstitutes the tragedy. He gives grief lessons their lessons.

You do not know who I am, says the child, who knows more than the child
says.

The Director apologizes for the stench of his knowledge.

God appears to be saying something. Why don't you try speaking to this object quadrifrontally?

The child organizes a retrospective on language.

The Director is called in to write the opening.

Instead he writes a resignation letter: *From line to line, we lived together.*

Language dismantles the dwelling.

[ ]

In the room / trying on clothes / the three girls / straighten their shirts / and part their hairs / What Must Change / in the mirror / a mustard of body / they have nothing to say to each other / who speaks in poetry / I have nothing to say to them / except the distance / one must not forget / I won't talk / can never be a colorless matter / I just want to move my hair / from one side / to the Other / in staggered language / and see my reflection   change

[ ]

My concept and your concept were in an argument. My concept said to yours

Regarding the bird feeder, you'll make them lose their foraging habits. My habits outweigh my desires at a ratio

The train comes slowly into the station

And something for not reading the news and something for saying I'd read *Things Fall Apart* when I hadn't

How the jasmine fills the room like a carousel of light I lay my head near

But I created the flower of chronic shame—watch it bloom

She said, I had a heart to heart with mom and things aren't

Because the earth is much bigger. Shame is much bigger. See the migration of caribou across northern Canada. 6,000 miles

If I could just measure exactly

And the next stop on this train

Or the male penguins storing eggs all darkwinterlong

My concept bought me flowers from Sunny's on 1st and 6th with a raffia bow

He said, but now you have your MFA

And the sparrow sat on the roof because it couldn't get in

Water in the station. Water in the lungs. One of the side effects. All the side effects on this train. If we pooled them together, we'd have a savings program

Only they were dried flowers

In an effort to place a word beside another word. Build

Put my hand in and draw the blood, little pieces of cranberry could-have-been

The constant action at the birdfeeder. In the wind spinning the cord. I want to see the small house crash against our window, see the glass separate

The will to disappear is a constant

Caribou of shame

They came round again battering their wings into the glass. The sparrow perched below on the fire escape, waiting for the seeds to drop

She said, your lights have gone out maybe because you're sick

I've forgotten how to do this, one foot in front of the other word

Time-lapse video of the cherry blossoms opening in Japan, the Okavango
Delta filling with water

Close-up of the elephant calf blinded by

Constant contact with the will to

NOTES

It's a place to live:
The poem is inspired by Marianne Moore's "The Steeple-Jack."

Kabul:
Each of the italicized headings refers to places in Afghanistan, and the poem includes several words in Dari (or Afghan Farsi), one of the main languages spoken in Afghanistan.

Bamiyan, in central Afghanistan, has traces of Afghanistan's Buddhist past, including the monumental Buddha statues blown up by the Taliban in March 2001.

Wardak is a province in the central eastern part of the country, and, because of its proximity to Kabul, has been a battleground throughout the wars.

Paghman, a town just outside of Kabul and popular as a weekend destination, is known for its garden and, according to the author's father, its magical bricks.

Mazar refers to the northern city Mazar-i-Sharif, which is the pilgrimage site of the Blue Mosque or the shrine of Hazrat-e-Ali, the cousin and son-in-law of prophet Muhammad. A "malang" is a dervish or a holy beggar. "Tarashak" is a homemade, flattened ice cream served with pistachios, almonds, and rose water, and is a specialty of the area.

Qargha is a large reservoir near Kabul where families frequently go for picnics.

Panjsher is located in the northeastern part of the country. In Dari, the valley name *Panjsher* means *five* ("panj") *lions* ("sher"). The word for "poem" is also "sher," though spelled differently. The military and political leader Ahmad Shah Massoud was known as the *Sher-e-Panjsher*, or the *Lion of Panjsher*. He was killed by al-Qaeda agents on September 9, 2001, two days before 9/11. Before being rebuilt into a larger monument, his original tomb was marked with a small, green-roofed structure.

father is on the tongue:
The Peshmerga is the official military force of Iraqi Kurdistan. Peshmerga literally translates to "before death," meaning "those who go before death."

"Veselka" is the name of a longtime Ukrainian restaurant in the East Village in New York City.

Haverhill refers to a street in West Palm Beach, Florida, and St. Mary's is the hospital where the author's father received radiation treatment for stomach cancer.

"peh yaw sheen meem ray gawf hay" is the transliterated Dari spelling of Peshmerga.

Who is this boy in the bone sac asking what to do?:
The following line is taken from Iranian poet Sohrab Sepehri's poem, "Water's Footfall": *I have a mother better than a blade of grass / friends better than flowing water.* The translation from Farsi is slant and the author's own.

Salaam alaikum:
The poem alternates between greetings in Dari and in Bambara, one of the main languages spoken in Mali, where the author traveled for work.

a word is legged:

Lady Sale or Florentina Sale (d. 1853) was the wife of British army officer Sir Robert Henry Sale and joined her husband on his post in Afghanistan during the First Anglo-Afghan War (1839-1842), part of the "Great Game," or the 19th century rivalry between the British and Russian empires over Central and Southeast Asia. In 1841, she was part of a group of people taken hostage by military leader Wazir Akbar Khan (son of Amir Dost Mohammad Khan), who opposed British occupation. Lady Sale kept a diary of the ordeal and in 1843 published it in England under the title, *A Journal of the Disasters in Afghanistan, 1841-2.*

"The Graveyard of Empires" is a moniker given to Afghanistan based on the claim that no foreign power has ever colonized the country.

Zbigniew Kazimierz "Zbig" Brzezinski (d. 2017) served as President Jimmy Carter's National Security Advisor from 1977 to 1981. Brzezinski was vehemently anti-Communist and the architect behind the CIA's collaboration with and arming of the Afghan Mujahideen against the Soviets, which led to the rise of the Taliban, later the development of al Qaeda, and the now the longest US war. In an interview in 2010, Brzezinski said, "The fact is that even though we helped the Mujaheddin, they would have continued fighting without our help.... They just happen to have a curious complex: they don't like foreigners with guns in their country. And they were going to fight the Soviets. Giving them weapons was a very important forward step in defeating the Soviets, and that's all to the good as far as I'm concerned."

We have lorded over nature and *Tell us about your violence and its relativism*: Both were both written while listening to *Democracy Now!* and drawing language from the airwaves.

ACKNOWLEDGMENTS

I am deeply grateful to Black Lawrence Press, especially Kit Frick and Diane Goettel, for plucking this out of the ether and then so lovingly crafting it into object.

To the editors of the following publications, who first published some of the poems in this collection, sometimes in earlier bodies and with titles: *Bone Bouquet, Brooklyn Rail, dOCUMENTA, Drunken Boat, Dusie,* and *elsewhere literary magazine.*

To Yolandi Oosthuizen for the lush art and every thoughtful, heartful step toward it.

To my tribe and mentors at Brooklyn College for casting the first light, and tenderly.

To the communities that have warmed and grown me: Afghan American Artists & Writers Association, Women of Color Writers' Workshop, Asian American Writers' Workshop, Kundiman, Blue Mountain Center, Home School, CUNY, Hampshire College, City Lore, and the countless rooms of daily surrender.

To my friends and loved ones, for joining in the hole and laughing on the ground and all manner of standing with.

Most of all, because first of all: To my padar jan, madar jan, Shabnam, Sahara, and Jawad—not language enough. And, always always always and alottle, to my lief and nafas, Nico.

Photo: Krista Fogle

Sahar Muradi is a writer, performer, and educator born in Afghanistan and raised in the U.S. / is co-editor of *One Story, Thirty Stories: An Anthology of Contemporary Afghan American Literature* / is co-founder of the Afghan American Artists and Writers Association / is recipient of the 2016 Stacy Doris Memorial Poetry Award and twice recipient of the Himan Brown Poetry Award / is a Kundiman Poetry Fellow and an AAWW Open City Fellow / directs the poetry programs at City Lore / and dearly believes in the bottom of the rice pot. Visit her online at saharmuradi.com